all things small

bathed in light
the dust flecks sparkle —
beauty hangs in the balance

Also by Susan J. Atkinson

The Birthday Party, The Mariachi Player and The Tourist / Catkin Press / 2021 / Second printing 2023

The Marta Poems / Silver Bow Publishing / 2020

all things small

all things small

Susan J. Atkinson

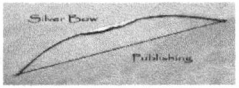

720 Sixth Street, Unit #5
New Westminster, BC
V3L 3C5
CANADA

all things small

Title: all things small
Author: Susan J. Atkinson
Publisher: Silver Bow Publishing
Cover Art: "On Land and Sea" by Susan J. Atkinson
Cover Layout and Design: Candice James

All rights reserved including the right to reproduce or translate this book or any portions thereof, in any form without the permission of the publisher. Except for the use of short passages for review purposes, no part of this book may be reproduced, in part or in whole, or transmitted in any form or by any means, either by means electronically or mechanically, including photocopying, recording, or any information or storage retrieval system without prior permission in writing from the publisher or a licence from the Canadian Copyright Collective Agency (Access Copyright).

www.silverbowpublishing.com
info@silverbowpublishing.com
ISBN: 978-1-77403-271-8- paperback
ISBN: 978-1-77403-272-5 electronic book
© Silver Bow Publishingb2024

Library and Archives Canada Cataloguing in Publication

Title: All things small / Susan J. Atkinson.
Names: Atkinson, Susan J., 1964- author.
Identifiers: Canadiana (print) 20240328051 | Canadiana (ebook) 20240328094 | ISBN 9781774032718
   (softcover) | ISBN 9781774032725 (Kindle)
Subjects: LCGFT: Poetry.
Classification: LCC PS8601.T565 A79 2024 | DDC C811/.6—dc23

all things small

for my parents, Donald and Margaret,
who taught me to find beauty
in all the small things

and for Anthony and our girls
with much love

all things small

all things small

Contents

love

This Love Poem Is for You / 13
The Way the Light Lies / 14
Pearl / 15
Geraniums / 16
Love Letters / 17
A Better Word for Yellow / 18
Kiss Me Again Like the Second Time / 19
A Peony, a Sun and a Moon / 20
As Sunlight Tilts on Its Axis / 21
In This We Find Ourselves / 22

sorrow

Counting Swans / 27
Driving West to Say Goodbye / 28
half moon full / 30
Sanctuary / 32
Signs Sneak Up on Small Feet / 33
How Can Things Die on a Morning Such As This / 34
The Pathology of a Garden / 35
This Past Month / 36
August / 37
The Colour of Mo(u)rning / 38
This Moon / 39
The Day After We Bring Your Ashes Home to England / 40
Cucumbers / 41
To You, Small Bird / 42

memory

Blackbird Singing / 45
The Clock She Drew / 46

Shirt, Brown, Honesty / 47
She Steals Silver Spoons from the Dining Room
          at the Home / 48
My Mother Looks for My Father in the Garden / 49
Home / 50
A Storm of Blackbirds Flaps in Her Brain / 51

divorce

Lessons, Part I / 55
Unstitching / 56
Adultery / 57
Magpie / 58
Infidelity / 59
To the boy who at one point may have been a lover / 60
Exhausted / 61
even today / 62
Catharsis / 63
Letting Go / 64
Lessons, Part II / 65
When You Find Yourself Alone in a Surrealist Painting / 66

all things small

To the Poet at the Table / 69
My Father, Having Been Invited to the Rich-People-down-
     the-Street's House for Dinner, Has a Story to Tell / 71
Pickling / 73
On Koh Phi Phi / 74
Jealousy / 75
Overindulgence / 76
The Dining Room Poem by Another Poet / 77
On Caye Caulker / 78
Open the Window / 79
Interpreting Rothko / 80
On a Spring Afternoon I Write Poems
     with My Class of Four-Year-Olds / 81
Something Beautiful / 82
Things That Never Come Back / 83

all things small

To the Sparrows Living in My Eaves / 84
April 2020 / 85
New Year's Day, 2022 / 86
Breathe / 87

Acknowlegments / 89

Author Profile / 91

all things small

all things small

love

all things small

This Love Poem Is for You
(for Anthony)

For you who sat at the bar in a downtown club.
For you who willingly accepted my spontaneous
tequila-fuelled fearless kiss.

For you who convinced me to remarry
that late December night when soft snow
settled in halos on streetlights below,
whose winter glow snuck through frayed shades
as we wrapped presents to put under the tree.

For you who encouraged me to rise
with the pinking of the sky to reach
the dangling string of a dream
and to hold it long enough to believe it.

For you who held me through loss,
lifted me through joy, anchored my way,
surprised me with the small things —
a favourite drink, a favourite book,
a late-night cheese-and-onion sandwich.

For you whose touch is heat and keeps me young.

The Way the Light Lies

A piece of sun-
   light lithe and limber
      lifts palm fronds
         at whim
            green fingers
tangled in late afternoon.

Oh, to have
   its confidence
      the way it clings
         and climbs around
            what it loves
no fear of appearing possessive.

That clever puppeteer
   stretching along
      your skin
         manipulating your spine
to meet its touch

and the casual way
   it so easily detaches
      without a glance
         leaving a shadow trailing
a step or two behind.

Pearl

I test your skin
as I would a pearl
sucking smoothness
to judge its quality —
my tongue threads
across the fabric
of your being
gliding gently over
sweet dewed sweat
your delicate nectar
testimony that you are
more precious than if
I had tasted salt.

all things small

Geraniums

The small petals crouched beside the dark green
curtain of summer cedar are past their best.

Their edges are crimped and browned
like the fringes of burned paper, a descent

into death accelerated by battering rains,
their remnants leaving a scent of sweet

tobacco rising from velvet puffy leaves.
Scent and memory — honeymoon in Paris,

where window boxes on every balcony
overflowed with vermilion crowns toppling

ablaze on skinny stems and you
and I wrapped in the scorch

of a midday siesta in a tiny hotel room,
three floors up a spiralling stairwell

the heat suffocating, air drenched
with the thick breath of geraniums.

Love Letters

I carry you
pressed in my pocket

like a handkerchief
kept just in case

my dashed ego needs
to be daubed

soothed or reminded
I was once held dear.

I use you and reuse you
bruised feelings wiped warm

by wisps of tender love —
lace held only by threads

which I wash and re-fold
into a neat little square

safely tucked away
until needed again.

A Better Word for Yellow

Rain skitters in the trees,
keeps us stitched to the deck.

You suck on peach flesh
fling the pip over the rail —

an open heart discarded. I watch,
tell you I want to write about love,

start with a peach and its yellow
sticky juice on your fingers.

I wrestle with yellow —
there must be a word

that says yellow better
than yellow. I give up

only to get stuck on peach and
how Eliot sort of took that one.

all things small

Kiss Me Again Like the Second Time

I ask you to tell me what you remember about our first kiss.
I tell you it's for a poem. Be poetic, I say, but no clichés.
Don't mention fireworks, or waves crashing on a sandy beach.
No talk of moths tempted by late-night light,
or choirs of angels singing.

You begin with the foot-race dare
down the middle of the snow-licked street.

You remind me of stopping at the intersection
to measure our height,
how our bodies seamlessly threaded into one another's,
how we lingered in the damp cold of December,
reluctant to say goodbye, reluctant to break the magic.

I remind you no clichés, adding my memory of how it felt,
the small of my back pressed against the driver's door
of your burgundy Altima, which we traded a year later
when we blended our families.

You remind me of your left hand
holding the back of my head,
smoothing my hair from the whip of wind,
your right light on my hip, your lips gentle against mine,
like rose petals bursting in air.

I let the clichés slip into quietness,
hold the rest against my heart.
All these years later, having never known before today
that you also think of our second kiss
with the fondness of a first,
I ask you to kiss me again like the second time;
the first was for dramatic effect.

A Peony, a Sun and a Moon

Suppose all that remains is the delicate scent
of a single white peony picked this morning,
its pink-edged petals
fluted like swan feathers
into a final curtsy.

Today the sun and moon
share the sky,
companionable in silence.
The sun coaxes early blooms
to open their pursed lips,
while the moon, full and tired,
rests in blue-tinged clouds.

Suppose all that remains
is a peony, a sun and a moon.
Could love be born of these three,
each carrying the weight
of their own beauty?

Remember how I always
picked those first blooms
for the dining room table?
The children's delight
when tiny ants would appear
unabashedly promenading from
petal to stem to dinner plate?

The sun in those days cast
leaf-dappled shadows
around the children,
the rush of conversation
each daughter tripping over
words to tell of her day.

And at night even with
blinds closed, every phase
of the moon lit our way.

all things small

As Sunlight Tilts on Its Axis

Morning welcomes winter,
solstice air so cold that frost flowers

bloom inside the room.
There is no birdsong today.

Perhaps they sleep long into
the morning, as you do,

hidden beneath blankets.
Today sunlight tilts

in a certain way,
glances the grey stubble

of your unshaved beard,
silver speckles in the furrows

of your changing face,
older now but still my love.

This season swallows your desire,
blurs days into listless gloom.

Your passion lies fallow.
I cup any hint of light to share.

In a while I will wake you, bring
black coffee and news of this day.

Together we will rejoice
in the gleam on tufts of fresh snow

and with whispered voices
wish winter well, while

hoping for the quick return
of daylight and warmth.

all things small

In This We Find Ourselves

As summer turns her back, buttoning
                          her coat to meet fall,
we escape to our cottage in the woods
                          at the top of a lane.

A recent illness has slowed your pace,
                        shrunk your bones
so your shadow now dawdles, falling
                          a step or two behind.

While you convalesce, gathered in blankets
                          that hem you to the porch,
I spend long hours wandering the woods, breathing the trees.

No longer a lost babe, I have learned these woods
                        and the years that grow around us.

My hair piled into a messy bun
              invites feathers and grasses to poke through;

the stray white strands — a nest fit for starlings to rest in.
I collect twigs and pebbles, frayed birch bark
                        pale as oysters,

small treasures to set around our table. I fashion teacups
                                    from acorn caps,
crochet bowls from half-bloomed clusters
                            of Queen Anne's lace,

imagine them
        filled with fresh-picked blueberries
                            and clouds of cream.

These are some of the things that will keep you well.
                  The way the light warms your shoulder,
        how patience and tenderness handclasp
                around whom we have become.

all things small

The trees that hid our lovemaking
                when our children were young
        shake rain-bruised leaves,
            catch the wind in song,
      a thousand tinkling tambourines.

At dusk we make friends with a wild rabbit,
              eat gingerbread dipped in milky tea

and when we tuck ourselves in for the night,
           the moon slips
          through a slit in the curtain,
     silvering a trail of scattered breadcrumbs
                  leading to our door.

all things small

all things small

sorrow

all things small

Counting Swans

On a trip to Toronto my child becomes
obsessed with counting swans.

Everywhere we walk along the harbourfront,
she counts them.

I tell her that they find a mate for life
and fall in love.

She wants to know if that is true,
then why is there an odd number?

I can only think of one explanation,
but it's sad

and reminds me of a funeral
years before.

My friend was the first to pass
in his family of twelve.

His mother and father led the processional,
the father wheeling the mother in her chair.

Their children followed in pairs,
the youngest without his partner.

Today it is spring and I do not want to talk about death.
Count them again, I say.

all things small

Driving West to Say Goodbye

March has come and gone.
It has mirrored our grief and pressed cold palms
against our sad slack faces.
We drive west to say goodbye.

Along this stretch of straight grey road
we have travelled so many times,
granite winks as winter runoff slips between rocks,
fool's gold polished by the sun.

Your mother has promised each of our girls,
her granddaughters,
a gem from her jewellery collection,
each carefully chosen to suit.

Emerald for the eldest, sapphire for the second,
topaz for the third
and for the youngest, a piece of tiger's eye
to match her wild spirit,

which your mother says was her as a child.
Our girl takes great delight in thinking
she could be like her grandmother,
who once paid a neighbour's boy to play the piano
during her lesson while she climbed out a window,
soft notes trailing as she ran into the afternoon.

In the warmth of the car I close my eyes and for a moment
I see starlings like black stencils against my lids.
I blink, they float like ash.

During these days of loss, the rain is heavy on our bones.
Our lovemaking has lapsed into a need to cling
and be close ... yet alone.

Through the long drive, silence pools,
so when we do speak, soup spoons dig into the air,
ladling our words, cradling them in silence.

all things small

At the house we make lists of all that will need to happen.
We drink champagne from Argentina, toast your birthday,
eat *piragi* and *klingeris*.

When it is time, we navigate our way home
under a sky mottled with stars,
pinpricks of silver dot quiet air,
everything feeling smaller than before.

half moon full

There is no cure, but we can trick ourselves on a warm
mid-April Saturday afternoon that the doorbell's ring
will bring a tall man in a black overcoat carrying a bag
of miracles ready for sale, or if not a tall man

we can believe it is a beautiful woman, in a long cape
with a pretty hood, selling combs to dress your
thinning hair and a basket of scarlet apples, one bite
to put you into a deep sleep, free from pain.

But it's not a tall man in a black overcoat or
a beautiful woman in a long cape, it's the young
children next door looking for permission to rescue
their ball, which has bounced onto your front lawn.

We sit in the living room surrounded by pockets of
quiet as you rest on your right side, shoulder pressing
into thin cotton sheets, white daisies squashed
beneath your weight, dust pinned in sunlight.

Bent bones of dying orchids hang from all the windows;
tired and grey, they thirst for a simple drop of water.
You are too sick to care for them now, but it is still
your house and we do not wish to overstep.

You spend your days counting full moons, always looking
forward, a silent wish for more time, another birthday,
another trip to the cottage. One more morning to watch
hummingbirds drink from the feeder you'd built years earlier.

We promise in a month we'll be there, sweeping floorboards,
freeing them of dead ladybirds and mice droppings,
but for now we must leave to make the long drive home,
and by night we find ourselves pulled by a low crescent.

all things small

When we stop for a break our daughter collects pinecones
from the roadside — childhood treasures to ease her fears
and in the silence, we tuck grief into small dark spaces
along with hope that you will see this new moon ripen.

Sanctuary

a near-naked moon
           swaddled only in clouds
dangles from
           a black sky

while rain
           punches pearl-white fists
                    against a glass ceiling

we look
           for a new sanctuary

a word
           to brace you in these moments
                    we no longer understand.

all things small

Signs Sneak Up on Small Feet

There is a warning before a rainstorm —
the open cup of an upturned leaf,
a cluster of crows crowding,
dark branches ready for flight.

In my hands I feel the rain gather,
my skin stretches over the swell
of my thumb and my bones ache
to escape from under the tightness.

Some signs we understand,
but of final days, we have no clue
and cannot stop death
once it has started.

How Can Things Die
on a Morning Such As This?

When the crown of the sun
breaches the trees in the backyard
and a mug of lemon tea cools
on a table fashioned from a tree trunk,
it's hard to believe things can die.
But they do.

Look closely. Already, summer blooms
bend their heads, their brown-tinged
leaves hang tired like crepe paper.

This is how it happens:
a beloved parent dies,
soon the other follows.
Loss cradles the space
between heart and rib
and grief becomes a shadow,
shares its mo(u)rning with sorrow.

When the crown of the sun
breaches the trees in the backyard
and a mug of lemon tea cools
on a table fashioned from a tree trunk
and when the shadows are at their longest,
you can see them holding hands for comfort.

all things small

The Pathology of a Garden

It is time to coax the garden.
Bring it back from a long winter.
We start with the neighbour's climbing rose,
which has staggered over our fence,
the effort leaving it slumped and tired.

We are all tired, feeling like grass whittled by wind;
flattened by your illness, we look for hope,
      desperate for a cure.
A search begins amongst what is left of the perennials.

My neighbour hangs over the wooden slats to prune the rose,
shares home remedies with friendly chatter.
It is becoming easier to speak of sickness,
      to untangle sadness.

She suggests we plant herbs. Rosemary for tumours,
St John's wort for sleep, holy basil for stress.
Tells me, *'Sow rock salt to kill the weeds,
and sprinkle eggshells to keep away slugs.'*

I pull up clumps of last year's garden.
Clutch a bouquet of dead parsley.
'Plant more,' my neighbour says, *'it makes a great balm
to soothe a blister, a boil, abrasions under the skin.'*

I don't know whether to believe, but she, too, has suffered
loss, and would like a garden of green
rather than the wild brambles that have overtaken the tulips
and bearded iris, spring flowers that stutter
under the weight of death.

Three crows bray in baritone,
stab at leftover grapes drooping from vines.
Harbingers, perhaps, but we have stopped looking for signs.
We wouldn't be able to read them anyway.

This Past Month

As spiders waken
and their webs string
from gate post to post,
catching me in the early hours,
I lose things. My keys, my purse,
your parents, unexpectedly.

Our youngest daughter
collects small pebbles,
curled bark of birch trees,
rocks with eyes,
small things to bury loss.
We, too, look for ways.

We camp by our favourite lake,
seek comfort in early summer —
how sun darts between ripples of water,
how a heron lands close to shore,
strutting in the shallows of light.

The heron stays for days.
We name it as if
a loved relative,
and when it spreads
its wings to leave,
everyone waves and fusses.

August

I kill a spider

    by accident

sends me into despair

    I spend hours

mind breezing over

    buttercups and cowslips

childhood memories

    rogue yarrow has gone

wild in the garden

    I can't decide whether to

dig it up and name it *weed*

    or tame it and call it *flower*

you say *tame*

    decision made

The Colour of Mo(u)rning

Dark lashes fringe the clouds —
a storm on its way darkens sky
and deadens the melody of birds;
a hush lays its heavy hand
across the face of the sun.

This storm batters the gravel path
with sharp slaps of rain and
blackness turns leaves inside-out,
stains the aching limbs of pines
struggling to remain upright.

The colour of mo(u)rning
hangs lifeless in the air.
I want to love the way the rain
inks everything black. I used to —
the way it creeps over everything.
But a year of loss, a year of wearing

the same clothing has changed all that.
The day matches a dress I no longer want.

Memories pleated into wrinkles
shrink its hemline as it haunts
the back of the closet. Should it be
given away, handed down or kept —

the ghosts impossible to iron out.

This Moon

This first full moon since your passing
catches me by surprise. A gap in the curtain

reveals its misty grey fullness
blurred in the wintry night.

A snow squall like white sparrows,
swoops against its edges.

The stars crumble
as the storm rumbles by.

Silver dust turns to ink.
I pen words of love and sorrow,

fill mason jars with water,
leave them to collect the glow.

Outside I dress myself
in snow and moonlight

until clouds sweep the sky,
shadowing our sad house,

its shutters lowered like eyes
heavy-lidded with grief.

The Day After We Bring Your Ashes Home to England

I am exhausted from sleep
dream of my dead parents
and an airplane trip, to where,
I don't know — I never get that far.
I need to pack all my childhood
possessions, squeeze them into
a suitcase and a carry-on bag.
The suitcase is beige vinyl
with a huge silver buckle.
It belonged to my parents,
bought from Debenhams,
for when we emigrated.

Grief tumbles through the dream
as I sob over all the decisions
I need to make. What will I take?
What will I leave behind?
Some of the things
belong to my parents.
The burden presses heavy paws
on my chest. At some point
as I struggle to close the case
my parents join the queue of people
waiting to board. They disappear
and I lose them again.

Cucumbers
(for Abigayle)

I teach my middle daughter how cucumbers ease
swollen, puffy eyes. How miraculously the cool juice
from their centre reduces signs from the night before.

I see in her face
she is out late each night,
sleeps through the mornings.

In this year of loss, I have taken to crying in my sleep,
heaving sobs as I lean against various characters
in my dreams.
In the light, I wake heavy and worn,
beaten by emptiness.

It's March, soon time for cut tulips,
wrapped and ready to be bought.

A clear glass vase, simple and curved
will sit on the table and I will spend hours
daydreaming, watching waxy petals flop,
cups bending on unsteady stems.
I will think of something other than loss,
write something other than loss,
but for now, poems grow from seeds
and morning brings a pile of half moons,
peeled cucumbers, curled and dried,
strewn beside our beds.

To You, Small Bird

Some anniversaries are harder than others.
On the eve of yours, four years since
your death, I find a goldfinch lying
by the terracotta flowerpot.

I hadn't noticed the corpse
on my way into the house,
lunch bag slipping free,
coffee dripping from upturned cup,
my grip loosening
from the weight of the day.

It wasn't until later when the crooked
bone of evening's moon caught
my eye, dragging it to rest
on the bright yellow breast
of the bird frozen on its back,
twig legs poking the night sky,
claws hooked and grasping at cool air,
the shock of stilled beauty
instantly symbolic.

With no more thought I scooped
the tiny body onto a paper towel,
buried it under the garden steps.
A shallow grave, perhaps easy
for the prowling tomcat, who after dusk
will no doubt find the small remains.

Later as I closed the sliding door
I noticed the smallest wisp of
a feather stuck to the glass
where the finch had flown
not knowing what was on the other side.

all things small

memory

all things small

all things small

Blackbird Singing

As the years passed my parents developed the language of twins, a secret, strange language that only they could know.

It's like a bird losing feathers

It started as a chorus of unwavering patience that allowed my mother to repeat again and again and again questions and thoughts; even my brothers and I stopped listening as the words began to blend into sounds like the singing of a gospel — blackbirds flapping from a pie.

You see one float by

My parents renamed the everyday into their own vocabulary. They renamed the clouds and the leaves, which turn inside themselves before a storm. They renamed the berries that droop heavy from bushes in late August, the rosehips, the gooseberries, the blackberries and even the dandelions.

And there it goes — another word gone

These words from our childhood fermented like vatted wine that bubbled and popped
in the dining room they had built. Words lost as if they were never there. Together they made a language so they could speak through the holes in my mother's
memory and when she forgot this language too —

one language dies every fourteen days

my father made up a new one, something only they would know, spoken through the whisper of fingers on skin.

Lines in italics are from National Geographic, July 2012

The Clock She Drew

My father reads an article on cognitive ability
in a health magazine about Alzheimer's.
Following the doctor's program
he gives my mother nothing but
protein and coconut oil at every meal.
My father, having tried many cures,
prays this could be it.

Before he starts this unusual diet
he tests my mother by having her draw a clockface.
She cradles the pencil tentatively,
as if unsure of what it does, her lack of pressure
leaving only light marks on the paper.

Her clock is not really a clock at all.

Scratches like bird prints in sand
line the middle of the page.
There is no circle.
There are no hands.
My father thinks
this is a good place to start.

Two months later
he tests her again.
My mother looks thin,
having lost weight, but
the clock face remains the same.

all things small

Shirt, Brown, Honesty
(for Penny)

My mother flutters on the edge of her seat
as the social worker assesses her need for extra care.

Her eyes flash, two burning fireflies
pulsing light and dark as she flits in
and out of what it all means.

My brother and I plead for her to answer sensibly.
We want to jump in, answer for her —

The social worker is patient and kind,
clickety-clacks responses on her humming computer,
fingers buzzing like bees over keys,
recording information, landing on everything.

Partway through the swarm of questions
the woman tells my mother three words:

Boy.   Man.   Ball.

At some point during the meeting
my mother will need to recall
and regurgitate what she is told.

I have been waiting for this, but the words are different
from the ones my friend warned me about.
Over glasses of wine we had giggled,
of how we will remind each other:

Shirt.   Brown.   Honesty.

Our foolproof way to cheat on the Alzheimer's test.

My mother will not remember the words.
Will not even remember being told.
By the time she is asked again the nouns will
have slipped through the honeycomb of her brain.

all things small

She Steals Silver Spoons from the Dining Room at the Home

We're driving through panels of April rain.
My father can't find their room key
and is fussing.
I pull over to help look —
the search leads to my mother's purse.

There is no key, but packaged carefully
are six silver spoons
nestled together,
stomach to back,
wrapped in white paper serviettes.

My father says my mother
does not know how to use utensils anymore.
Which one to use,
which hand to hold them.
Sometimes a fork for soup, a spoon for rice,
neither holding food long enough to reach her mouth.

I wonder what she must have thought
while taking the spoons.
Was she hiding the wretched tools?
Did she think they would make a pretty collection
and take them as a child might?

When I was young, I stole
a coin from the dining room sideboard.
I didn't know it was a Deutsche Mark
until I tried to spend it on sweets —
all I had seen was *shiny*.

Perhaps that's what my mother saw.

She doesn't know anything about the spoons
but insists if she'd had the key it would not be lost.

all things small

My Mother Looks for My Father in the Garden

My mother looks for my father in the garden
finds herself swamped by Queen Anne's lace
and can't remember what she's doing

stands naked

sun's heat a serpent's tongue
uncoiling along
every inch of skin

waltzing swallows
stencil shadows
across her bare chest

she murmurs
with the birds
grief lies in her bones

she spends hours hugging trees
scraping the insides
of her curved arms

scarlet lines scratched on skin
his name bitten
into the ribs of her tongue

Home

Most days she does not know where she lives,
the halls and corridors an unfamiliar maze.

Carnation-sized bruises bloom on the back of her hands
from bumping into door frames, tripping over carpet edges.

I bring her home for a night, dress her in gloves and boots,
it's growing cold for September.

I worry: Will she sleep?
In those early weeks after he died, she would wake

hour after hour, wander along our landing,
open our bedroom door, searching for him.

Tonight, I sleep on an old army cot beside her,
wake with every movement, reach out before she rises.

She tells me she doesn't want to live here
even though she doesn't know where here is.

I ask if she could live anywhere, where
would it be. She wants to be with him again.

She wants to go home.

For breakfast I cut grapefruit into half moons,
sprinkle sugar, cut around the edges of the fruit.

I am careful not to pierce the skin
where sweetness could seep through its pith.

A Storm of Blackbirds Flaps in Her Brain

the exam
shirt
brown
honesty

her songbirds gossip
lost nouns
scrabble
through air

tuesday clouds spit
daisy petals
the rainstorm sweet
she doesn't remember lunch

the clock
bird's feet
patterned
in pencil dust

a cluster of lily pads
mouths yawning
guzzle river water
she can't remember names

the weight of summer
tips balance
in the second cutting
of hay, she remembers the smell

the wisp of wind
catches birch leaves
a sound she spent
her life trying to describe

all things small

all things small

divorce

all things small

Lessons, Part I

I have learned
to part the air
with my arms when I run.

I have learned
that not all
flowers bloom.

I have learned
to pick up
broken glass carefully.

And I have learned
that with enough space
things move in between.

Unstitching

words loop like stitches

from a needle

knit one

too much said

purl one

we decrease the pattern

drop one

soon a gaping hole

between us

Adultery

Adultery skulks in
like a cat
through a crack
in a door.
Its tail gently curves
like a question mark,
dark and heavy.

It appears unannounced
seeking attention —
a cat that I do not wish
to touch or hold
(cats always go to those
who are allergic).

Adultery slips in,
like a cat begging
to be caressed
and stroked,
a question
needing answers
to complete a sentence
and close the door.

Magpie

The magpie who stole my wedding ring
and fucked my husband had dark wings

and blue eyes speckled with
saccharin like candy Easter eggs.

The magpie wrapped her long fluttering
tail feathers around him while her lips

coated in berry juice blew hot
promises in rapid whispers.

Me, I was shoved into the shadows
where time passed and frigid winds

tarnished and cheapened the ring
(once so golden and appealing).

Funny how things turned out — because
I'd now lost interest and as you might guess

the magpie who stole my wedding ring
had also lost interest and spat it out

for a brighter, more opulent bauble.

Infidelity

spit spot
lip shine
your lips
on mine
bare
table bare
age-cracked
stains stare
into blank

space

between

us

stains remember
lip stain — stains my lips
I feel hers on yours through mine

To the boy who at one point may have been a lover

Dear Maybe,

This is just to say
I found the letters

you wrote
thirty years ago

at the bottom
of an old shoebox

underneath birth, marriage and
divorce certificates

and all kinds of other papers

*I was probably
saving them just in case*

I wonder now
what may have happened

if I had visited that weekend
all those years ago

perhaps it would have been
delicious and sweet.

all things small

Exhausted

Exhaust fumes seep
through the tiny crack
where the moulding
has rotted around
the window frame.

      I
    gasp
   surely
      I

can't die from
carbon monoxide poisoning
through a closed
(well, almost closed)
window.

all things small

even today

on
the
last day
of summer when
the trees shiver scarlet
shaking changing leaves
even today with a sun so soft
and muted and dressed for fall
even today I can not find
words to form a poem
I can not think of
anything worth-
while to say
...
e
v
e
n

t
o
d
a
y

all things small

Catharsis

It is late in the fall,
cold for October

    I have let the garden go
(too busy, too worried,
too distracted)

the overripe, overgrown climbers
    wither their leaves a diaphanous green,
collapse from signs of early frost

    I pull up vines
uprooting anger
    throw tomatoes
bulging with the weight of summer

    send them bouncing
against the garage wall

       fast pitch
       slow slide
       skin bursting
       seeds spilling
       with each smash
       red fades

and I am soothed
    little by little
        piece by piece

Letting Go

rearranging cupboards and drawers
glasses placed where the plates used to go

sleeping naked tangled in sheets
the pillows scattered

walls of a fort collapsed
the bed no longer divided

pulling down the past
crumbling dried rose petals

bunched brittle memories smelling of age
and death and too much past life clenched in their grasp

neatly packing unwanted items
ready for the garbage

Lessons, Part II

I have learned
to tiptoe gently
in soft snow.

I have learned
to take corners
slowly.

I have learned
the rosebush will die
if not covered in winter.

And I have learned
to pretend the lover
in my dreams is you.

all things small

When You Find Yourself Alone in a Surrealist Painting

That sound you don't recognize,

it's the trees whispering, watching the sun uncoil orange
along your skin. Trees bending their heads close

telling tales to the neighbours. You are alone and would
join the chatter if you spoke their language.

Farther around the bend, grass ignores, still and silent,
not interested in gossip.

You swallow autumn, scarlet crunching in the gap
between lips and teeth.

A black dress trembles in the air, long and thin like a ribbon,
but it's not a dress, it's crows careening toward trees,
called by the rustling that you don't understand.

Nothing makes sense but the quilt of the sky,
the way it always was, on outings,
when you picked apples, everything

sharp red, souring the tongue, green shading
of not-quite-ripe in the basket
and everyone posing for photographs,
white-teeth-wide-smiles

no room to be alone.

all things small

all things small

all things small

all things small

To the Poet at the Table

The poem I'd been trying to write
left my pen
only to resurface,
days later,
clinging to the chandelier wire

well out of reach.

It swung
loose-limbed and leggy,
from crystal teardrops plump with dust.
My fingers grasped
at its lines,
now so far away
I couldn't even remember what they were.

Gone, I thought, until one day
the poem popped up unexpectedly
at dinner.

Afraid to startle it
I sat patiently
as it busied itself
between wine glasses,
clambered over cutlery
and stumbled over plates
to rest at your elbow.

I watched that poem
and I
noticed how
you left the table
long after everyone else
as if you were looking for something.

I noticed how
your fingers chattered through crumbs
carelessly dropped

all things small

as if you were searching for the taste
of a word
among the specks left,
perhaps hoping for a morsel of conversation
to savour for later.

I noticed how
you spat back the bits you didn't want,
bland clichés, watery and over-chewed.

I also noticed how,
when you did leave,
you took
a small bag of leftovers,
a collection of undigested scraps

and it was then I realized
the poem I'd been trying to write
had reappeared
in the restless flutter of your fingers
amongst the debris of dinner,
which you collected
and put in the bag
probably to save
for a poem of your own.

all things small

My Father, Having Been Invited to the Rich-People-down-the-Street's House for Dinner, Has a Story to Tell

Back then sixteen was leaving age, coming of age,
and so, my father was considered a man, not a boy,
when invited to dinner for the first time,
to his (at the time) girlfriend's house.
Back then in a class system flourishing to ripeness,
this girl and her family were certainly perching
on a higher rung of the ladder,
and because at this particular time my father was anxious
to please and impress, he wore his Sunday best
that late summer evening.
He made the right sounds, cocked his head
in that jaunty way that speaks interest
and answered all questions with a much smoother tone than
what was familiar to his slightly common accent.

His girlfriend preened proudly as the family enjoyed
the fresh-faced young man's company —
my father, after all, despite lack of money and status
was well brought up and nicely educated
(he would become a pioneer in the world of computers),
but on this particular evening around this particular table
he found himself choosing to do something quite unexpected.

A salad had been served,
back then a delicacy mostly for the rich,
and certainly something new for a Northern working-class lad.
How grand the platter must have seemed with sliced eggs
cut like teardrops edging perfectly rounded slices of radish,
the pink bleeding into white like the frilly hem of a party frock.
Blobs of salad cream and ovals of cucumber,
small boats in a sea of red cabbage
and in the centre, a bed of lettuce, crisp green leaves
cushioning — curled and relaxed — a caterpillar.

all things small

Now what was my father to do? Back then
pointing out the furry fiend would surely risk suggestion
the cook had not done her job, yet leaving the food
on his plate would perhaps imply his unsophisticated palate
did not like something that to this family was pretty basic fare.
These thoughts must have tumbled over one another,
resting on what really was his only choice.
With the correct knife and fork poised
in both of his hands my father rolled the caterpillar
in its blanket and popped it in his mouth.

As it turned out my father never went
to the rich people's house for dinner again.
Not because he had not been the ideal guest,
but rather for his own twist of fortune.

As it turned out, several nights after the caterpillar incident
the rich girl caught a cold and missed the Sea Cadets' dance
where my father would meet my mother.

Pickling

We sit on the kitchen floor, black and white linoleum squares
faintly cracked, flecked grey, camouflaging dirt.

You teach me how to pickle onions. Perfect white balls
lined with spider veins, picked from your garden.

You pass the time telling stories about my grandmother,
who, as a child, worked in a pickle factory, her job to stand

in the yard plucking pickles from a tub of brine,
small swollen hands scooping and searching in icy,

stinging water. At the end of each day she would soothe
her raw red fingers in the heat under her aunt's armpits.

I couldn't imagine her as a girl. All I could remember
was a tired old woman, brown with age,

lying on the couch, I by her side as she told and
retold the story of The Three Billy Goats Gruff.

Her whispered croak, a breath against my cheek,
her bristled chin wagging loosely with each word

and me at five years old scared into stillness, wondering
if she might have been the troll under the bridge.

On Koh Phi Phi

In the late afternoon after the rain
that falls from a hole in a cloud
in the dark storm grey of sky

leaves everything so sticky and hot
that kerosene stains from the fire show
the evening before bubble on the beach

and at four o'clock the tide drains for the day
as if a plug has been pulled, leaving long-tail boats
stranded on damp patches of sand for the night

a young German falls in love with a stranger
a beautiful girl whose hair trickles like ribbons of
licorice as she walks out of the empty ocean

the young man drinks with her late into the night
follows her through the winding streets
gets a matching tattoo fashioned after a Hollywood star

and the next day changes his ticket
decides he doesn't want to leave
visits her room to tell her, but it is vacant

except for a row of black ankle socks
hanging like bats and the bracelet
he bought for her the night before.

Jealousy

Jealousy can do more than slither under the skin.
It can appear on the doorstep late in the night,

in the middle of a dinner party, ready to hold hands
with Indulgence, whose good cheer has left the other

guests sitting too close, saying too much,
seeing things not as they are.
Jealousy shows up as martinis trip on tottery stems,

slinks in, garish in lime green, glint in the eye,
looking for trouble
(funny how it takes its place quietly, just as coffee is served),

slides in beside knives and napkins, waiting
like an after-dinner mint for the end of the meal
when so much has been said and done and

it can be popped into a willing mouth, sucked and smacked
between warm lips, smooth, round, the size of a pebble,

fitting under the tongue so the vile shade of envy spreads,
flavour clinging, wanting to be wanted,
wanting a partner for the night, to be held tight,
embraced and coddled, emerald prickles
brushing cheek to cheek, hot closeness bringing comfort

                and then;
Jealousy, having found its mate, is ready to be carried to bed.
Its taste lingers under the tongue,
splinters piercing tender skin.

Overindulgence

Overindulgence is never invited
to the dinner parties
down the street,
but somehow
    as night tucks around itself
and the other guests
start to leave,
it raps on the door
and breezily walks in.
    Of course, there are still
one or two around the table
eager to greet
laughing as the new arrival
tiptoes along the rims of glasses,
dipping where it doesn't belong,
    tripping onto open laps,
sharing secrets
that if shared further
will simply be blamed
on this latecomer.
    Funny how not long after
Overindulgence arrives,
Jealousy leaves with Hope
and Anger is left to clean up
the mess.

The Dining Room Poem by Another Poet
(for Deanna)

I read the poet's poem
about her dining table
the one where
the table is long and white where
the father flips when she speaks through the quiet.
Spaghetti fills the air
sauce spurting red across the floor
the mother on her knees mopping the mess
blood-like stains on a pregnant belly
and the poet at seven years old
feels teeth around her neck
from the points of her collar on a dress she loves.

I read the poem and imagine
how difficult it must have been to contain
her day's joy and how, when it did escape,
hiccupping into the scene,
she must have desperately wanted to scoop it off her plate
and push it deep down her throat
back where it had come from.

On Caye Caulker
(after "On Naxos" by Nicholas Christopher)

A blond boy/man with a ponytail
wearing a tattered moss-green T-shirt
smashes coconuts on a whittled stake;
his brown muscles bulge with the effort
and the palm trees are still
as he strips their innards into kernels
no bigger than a tennis ball.

Under the shadow of the fronds he harvests his treasure.
Sure of what he wants, he piles the rest,
the unwanted skins, high into a funeral pyre.

With kernels hoarded in a cloth saddlebag he walks away,
turning his back to the empty beach
and the birds clicking in the leaves,
their beaks snicking dried blades
that catch late-afternoon light.

And the white crescent moon
    balances precariously
  in the soon-to-be night sky.

Open the Window

open the window
unlock the door
the storm is biting
at the latch
fling open the windows
flip free the blinds
let the downpour
flood in

open the window
the tide is high
let slippery-slippered
rain rage
and wake
the cackle of
morning crows
fashioning shadows
on the walls

open the window
let the sky tumble in
and mid-autumn air
bite at our sheets
let the scythe of
a dying moon slice
our sleep and
rouse our dream-
soaked skin

Interpreting Rothko

Faced with a choice I am torn between
No. 8, 1953, Lilac and Orange over Ivory

and *Untitled, 1956*, which if I were
to name it I would suggest something like

Puffs of Snow or Sheep's Coat Sandwiched
between Charcoal and Ruby. I am sure

neither, in their softness, would suit Rothko
though my delicate musings

about the ivory would probably also fall flat:
its edges, a lathe frame around a window,

cutting blushed-peach ripeness of
sunset settling into the Aegean Sea

while miles below the cliffs, past the winding streets
of a Greek village, in the last of the light

paled to lilac strips, women weave olive branches
into fences that stop goats from pattering off rocky ledges

and the wind dies in a curtsied hush, barely audible
beneath the bold slabs of colour.

all things small

On a Spring Afternoon I Write Poems with My Class of Four-Year-Olds

A little boy who holds his pencil like a weapon
and cannot scribe his own name
tells me spring is like orange circles

lots of orange circles
that smell like his pockets
and never stop

and my little shy girl
whispers that the trees grow gold
and sing *wish, wish, wish*.

all things small

Something Beautiful *

On a cold November afternoon my class of six-year-olds
and I read the picture book *Something Beautiful*. We cry

for the elderly lady who lives on an alley-way doorstep
in a cardboard box. She is wrapped in a thick plastic

cape for warmth and in the background of the picture
shattered glass from a bottle sparkles like *fallen stars*.

On scraps of paper the children design a new home —
their something beautiful
for the old lady in the cardboard box.

Most draw castles and palaces with hearts and flowers
blooming from colourful walls, except my new student,

who was uprooted from Syria and coarsely planted here.
On his square of white paper
he draws what he knows about home.

A fighter jet shrieks through a grey sky darkened from the
pressure of his stubby pencil pinned to one spot.

Bombs drop on a row of roofs,
destroying all the houses but one.
My boy colours fiery smoke in diaphanous red.

Out of his paler grey wisps, a kaleidoscope of butterflies
burst and flutter above the destruction —

his something beautiful shaded mauve and blue,
yellow hearts emblazoned on each curved wing.

*Something Beautiful (Dragonfly Books, 2002)
by Sharon Dennis Wyeth

all things small

Things That Never Come Back

Once while teaching
a class of nine-year-olds
how to write a list poem
one boy wrote about things
that go and come back.

    Boomerangs, yo-yos, the tide.

I wanted him to stretch his thinking
so asked him to write
about things that go and
don't come back.

    His new poem had
    one line —

    my father.

To the Sparrows Living in My Eaves

Late winter and the clouds bloom white as you lay
your nest in the crease between the roof and eaves.

For a month or more I have watched you toil through
early-morning frost, a squabbling couple picking up

bits and bobs from the tangled remains of last year's garden.
I marvel at your strength.

A cedar clipping the size of a hand,
its green fingers flapping like extra wings
as you carry it to the roof.
I marvel at your determination
as the small cellophane wrapper
of processed Gouda cheese stubbornly sticks
to the thorns of the rosebush,
but you pick and pick until it is free to carry away.

I see the edges of the home you are building,
its intricate lacing holding it together,
keeping it wedged in a crack
worn from weather and neglect.

In these hours
the pleasure of watching you build
offsets the truth that you have probably caused
all kinds of damage,
judging by the tufts of pink insulation
that steadily snow down.

April 2020

spring has slowed
given up to a cold snap

the neighbour's ornamental grass
bends in a clumsy bow

battered from the storm
the clump clings to gardening string

that struggles to hold
the bundle together

no one is out today
too cold to sit six feet apart

the street rests
birds cease their chatter

the only sound — the scuffle
of a broken umbrella bullied

by the riffle of breath
as the wind exhales

New Year's Day, 2022

My foot claw-curls the edge
of the passing year.

This dark time that should
be easy to leave behind

rolls beneath my sole,
shifts balance and sand.

Fear has blanket-knitted
around our shoulders,

become a comfortable mantle
hard to shrug.

On a beach the sudden
breach of waves,

like the unknown, startles.
An unexpected spray flies

into the gasp of my mouth
opened by the surprise flight

of a graffitied bluebird
alighting from the harbour wall.

The bird spreads its thinly stencilled
tail feathers to the expanse of sky

the sweetness of hope
curves the o of my lips.

Breathe

Three weeks into our new reality
cars are idle, streets quiet.

From my brown couch
I watch the seasons shift.

Spring creeps on silent feet,
we barricade behind our doors.

In the breath of morning
I speak the sky.

Look for new words
to describe blue, and blush of sun.

Birds pirouette on rain-licked wires,
shifting from foot to foot to find balance.

Black city crow circles bare branches,
buries its neck against wind.

Woodpecker rat-a-tats
its beak between cracks

in the trunk of a linden tree
as a cardinal streaks

through the cedars,
adding its voice to the choir.

Laundry, forgotten on the line
quivers madly for attention,

while in the kitchen two of my daughters
bake banana bread with giant chocolate chips.

all things small

Beauty betwixt all the uncertainty of now,
a reminder to breathe

                breathe.

breathe.

                breathe.

Acknowledgements

Thank you to the journals and anthologies where a number of these poems first appeared: Artfest Anthology 2024, Apt613's Hope Anthology, *Arc Poetry Magazine, Bywords.ca, Byline,* The Canadian Authors Association's 20/20 Vision Anthology, *The Dalhousie Review, flo. Literary Magazine, Green's Magazine, In/Words Magazine,* The League of Canadian Poets' *Fresh Voices* and *Poetry Pause, ottawater,* The Peter F. Yacht Club Anthology, *Pinhole Poetry, Room Magazine, The Carleton Arts Review, The New Quarterly, Queen's Quarterly* and *White Wall Review.*

Thank you, also, to several selection and contest committees. **Kiss Me Again Like the Second Time** was named an honourable mention in *The New Quarterly*'s 2023 Nick Blatchford Contest. **Love Letters** was a contest winner in the 2022 North Grenville Poetry Contest. **Jealousy** won first prize in the Canadian Authors Association's 2019 National Capital Writing Contest and **Something Beautiful** was a finalist in the 2020 National Capital Writing Contest. **half moon full** won first prize in the 2016 Carleton University Literary Prize. **Driving West to Say Goodbye** was named an honourable mention in *Arc Poetry Magazine*'s 2016 Diana Brebner Contest.

My thanks to the Ontario Arts Council for grants that gave financial assistance while I was writing parts of this book. With gratitude, thank you to *Arc Poetry Magazine, Guernica Editions, Palimpsest Press* and *The New Quarterly* for seeing the potential and supporting the manuscript through the OAC's recommender grant program.

Gratitude to Candice James, publisher and editor, who continues to show unwavering support for my work and always, always, always makes me feel like I am her favourite poet.

Overwhelming thanks to my fellow poets from both my dear, dear Ruby Tuesdays writers group and the Other Tongues poetry group. Your continued expertise, passion, support and suggestions have helped more than words can say.

all things small

I offer my heartfelt thanks to David O'Meara, great mentor and friend, who patiently and kindly read the manuscript in all its drafts and helped shape the manuscript into the book that it is today. Thank you, thank you, thank you for your keen eye, fabulous feedback and endless support.

Huge thanks to editor and great friend, Margo LaPierre, for pushing the manuscript into its final stages of becoming the collection you are reading today. Much love and gratitude for your time, care and acute attention.

And it is with all my love that I thank my family — Anthony and our daughters Jasmine, Hayley, Abigayle and Tiah — and my amazing group of friends, who inspire me and hold me up when I feel down. An extra-special thanks goes to my beautiful Daisy Velvet Jayne, who held my hand through the long path of making this book a book. ☺ Thank you for listening tirelessly and for always finding a solution to every problem.

all things small

**photo courtesy of
Tiah Rose Lefresne**

Susan J. Atkinson is an award-winning teacher and poet born and raised in Northern England. After fifteen years working in the Toronto film industry, she now makes her home in Ottawa, Ontario, where she and her filmmaker husband have raised their four daughters. Her poetry has appeared in such journals as *Arc Poetry Magazine*, *The Antigonish Review*, *The Dalhousie Review*, *Grain Magazine*, *The New Quarterly*, *Queen's Quarterly*, and *Room Magazine*.

She was an Honourable Mention in The New Quarterly's 2023 Nick Blatchford Occasional Verse Contest and her suite, **Alice, Circa 1985** was long listed for Exile Edition's 2023 Ruth and David Lampe Poetry Award. She has also won the Carleton University Literary Contest and the Canadian Authors Association's National Capital Writing Contest, and a suite from **The Marta Poems** was shortlisted for *Exile Quarterly*'s Gwendolyn MacEwen Poetry Competition.

She also writes stories and poetry for children and is the author of four picture books published by Little Witch Press (www.littlewitchpress.com).

all things small is Atkinson's second full-length collection. Her debut, **The Marta Poems**, was published by Silver Bow Publishing in 2020. Visit www.susanjatkinson.com to find out more.

www.ingramcontent.com/pod-product-compliance
Lightning Source LLC
Chambersburg PA
CBHW052150070526
44585CB00017B/2060